Anonymous

Stranger's New Guide Through Boston and Vicinity

A complete handbook. Vol. 1

.

Anonymous

Stranger's New Guide Through Boston and Vicinity
A complete handbook. Vol. 1

ISBN/EAN: 9783337212940

Printed in Europe, USA, Canada, Australia, Japan

Cover: Foto ©Andreas Hilbeck / pixelio.de

More available books at **www.hansebooks.com**

ˈGERS' NEW GUIDE

THROUGH

BOSTON AND VICINITY.

A COMPLETE HANDBOOK,

DIRECTING VISITORS

WHERE TO GO,
WHEN TO GO,
AND HOW TO GO,

THROUGH THE CITY AND SUBURBS.

WITH NEW MAP OF BOSTON.

BOSTON:

JAMES R. OSGOOD AND COMPANY,

(LATE TICKNOR & FIELDS, AND FIELDS, OSGOOD, & CO.)

124 TREMONT STREET.

1872.

Price Ten Cents.

BOSTON ILLUSTRATED:

AN ARTISTIC AND PICTORIAL HANDBOOK

OF

BOSTON AND ITS SURROUNDINGS.

CONTAINING Full and Concise Descriptions of Objects and Scenes of Interest in Boston and Vicinity; with nearly One Hundred and Fifty Illustrations, expressly prepared for it.

☞ For full description, see third and fourth pages of cover.

JAMES R. OSGOOD & CO., Publishers,

124 Tremont Street, Boston.

MAP OF BOSTON.

1872.

WITH ALL THE LATEST IMPROVEMENTS.

A COMPLETE GUIDE TO STRANGERS.

Strangers' New Guide

THROUGH

Boston and Vicinity.

A COMPLETE HANDBOOK,

DIRECTING VISITORS

WHERE TO GO,

WHEN TO GO,

AND HOW TO GO,

THROUGH THE CITY AND SUBURBS.

WITH NEW MAP OF BOSTON.

BOSTON:

JAMES R. OSGOOD AND COMPANY,

(LATE TICKNOR & FIELDS, AND FIELDS, OSGOOD, & CO.)

124 TREMONT STREET.

1872.

PUBLISHERS' NOTE.

THIS Guide is based on "The Strangers' Guide," which has been published for several years; but it has been entirely re-written, and brought down to date, so as to include whatever would be of general interest to the residents of Boston, and to visitors attracted to the city by the World's Peace Jubilee. It is a full, compact, and clear index to the most noteworthy buildings, public works, views, drives, railways, and historical treasures of Boston and its suburbs, and is hardly less useful and convenient for residents than for strangers.

The references at the bottom of the pages are to "BOSTON ILLUSTRATED," a full Pictorial and Descriptive Hand-Book of the city and its surroundings, which describes and illustrates the topographical, architectural, and historical incidents of Boston and vicinity so fully and concisely as to include within a portable book a vast amount of curious and valuable information respecting the city and its environs. It is so handsome, useful, and cheap a work that no one interested in Boston and its history should be without it.

Entered, according to Act of Congress, in the year 1872,
BY JAMES R. OSGOOD & CO.,
In the Office of the Librarian of Congress, at Washington.

Rand, Avery, & Co., Stereotypers and Printers, 3 Cornhill, Boston.

CONTENTS.

HOW TO SEE BOSTON AND THE SUBURBS.

CONVEYANCES ABOUT BOSTON.

CONVEYANCES OUT OF BOSTON.

3

STRANGERS' NEW GUIDE

THROUGH

BOSTON AND VICINITY.

How to See Boston and the Suburbs.

BY HORSE-CARS AND RAILROADS.

We suppose the reader to be a stranger in Boston, to be entirely unacquainted with its crooked streets, and to require to be directed even from his hotel to any given point of departure for the various places of interest in and about the city. It will not, however, be difficult to find the three starting-points of the horse-car lines, namely: Scollay Square, at the junction of Tremont and Court Streets, Cornhill, and Pemberton Square; Park-street Church; and Bowdoin Square, at the junction of Cambridge, Green, Court, and Chardon Streets. It is proposed to indicate the routes to be taken by horse-cars, omnibuses, and ferries, or on foot for short distances, and afterwards to sketch a few drives into the neighboring country. Those who take private carriages to see Boston itself may follow the routes here described.

Engravings and Descriptions in " Boston Illustrated."

5

The Business Quarter.

In order to see the business part of Boston, one may trust to his own powers of pedestrianism after reaching Scollay Square. He should pass down Court Street, noticing on the right the Adams Express Office, the County Court House, and Sears Building, — the latter the finest edifice of the kind in the city, — and on the left two or three handsome granite structures, and the " Daily Advertiser " Building. On reaching Washington Street, turn to the left, and pass down into Dock Square, one of the oldest quarters in the city. A short distance farther in the same direction, and we reach Faneuil Hall, the famous " Cradle of Liberty," surmounted by the grasshopper vane, and, just beyond, the new Faneuil-hall Market, commonly known as Quincy Market. At the lower end of the market, we arrive at Commercial Street, with its elegant and substantial warehouses. Turning to the right, and following Commercial Street, we come to State Street. The granite building in the square is the Custom House; and it will well repay an examination. Facing down the street towards the water, we see the solid and imposing State-street Block of fifteen wide and high stores, — the best example in Boston of wholesale warehouses. Beyond this block is the new marginal Atlantic Avenue, which is to skirt the city on the water side. Facing in the opposite direction, we see the Old State House in the centre of the street, and are looking directly into the square where the famous Boston Massacre took place on March 5, 1770. On either side of the street are fine structures, some of them devoted to mercantile purposes, but the most to banking, insurance, lawyers', and brokers' offices, and the like. On the left are the central office of the Western Union Telegraph Company, and the Post Office, soon to be removed to the new building on Devonshire Street. We pass now in the rear of the Custom House into India Street, thence up Milk Street a short distance into Broad. In this section are the great wholesale grocery establishments. Passing through Broad to Oliver Street, thence up Oliver to High Street, we are now in the Fort-hill district, where a high hill covered with dwellings has been completely levelled, and will henceforward be devoted to business purposes. Passing through High Street, we come to Pearl, — a street devoted throughout its whole length to the boot-and-shoe trade, in which Boston takes the lead. We cross Congress Street a little farther on, and come to Federal Street, on both of which a very large business is done in wool, Boston being the head-quarters of that trade in the country. Continuing still on High Street, at Summer Street we come into the district devoted to dry goods. We pass up Summer Street between rows of very elegant and spacious stores. On the left is Chauncy Street, and on the right Devonshire Street, both given up to dry goods and clothing establishments. We take Devonshire Street, and crossing Franklin, which for its noticeable granite structures is probably unexcelled by any business street in the world, pass by the magnificent new Post-office to Water Street, and through the latter street to Washington. We have now made the circuit of the greater part of the wholesale district of the city. Nearly opposite Water is School Street, through which we now pass. On the right we see the magnificent City Hall and the ancient King's Chapel, and on the left the celebrated Parker House. On turning to the left into Tremont Street, we find on the right the Tremont House, a large and elegant stone-front hotel of the first class, the Granary Burying Ground, — the third established in Boston, — and Park-street Church. On the left are Tremont Temple, the Horticultural Hall, the Studio Building, and the publishing house of J. R. Osgood and Co. Winter Street, which comes into Tremont just below the head of the Common, is a great street for ladies' shopping ; and the Music Hall, containing the "Great Organ," is on a court just off Winter Street, on the left as one faces Washington Street. Next comes Temple Place, where are some fine business structures. We have meanwhile passed St. Paul's (Episcopal) Church, and the United States Court House, on the corner of Temple Place. Continuing still on Tremont Street, we pass the beautiful marble building occupied by the Mason and Hamlin Cabinet Organ Company, and come to the foot of the Common. Here we see several very fine buildings : on the north-east corner of Tremont and Boylston Streets is the Masonic Temple, dedicated in 1867 ; on the south-east corner is the Hotel Boylston, one of the most elegant French flat-hotels in the city, owned by the Hon. Charles Francis Adams; on the south-west corner is the Hotel Pelham, the pioneer in Boston of the "flat" system, and famous from having been moved back bodily twenty feet when Tremont Street was widened, without disturbing the occupants of the house ; the next building but one, passing down Boylston Street, opposite the Common, is the Public Library, to be mentioned again. Turning now away from the Common into Boylston Street, we reach Washington Street, and, turning to the left, we follow it to Cornhill. On the right we pass the Globe Theatre. A little farther on the left, we come to the fine building of the Mercantile Savings Institution and the Boston Theatre. We are now in the great retail district of the city. Several buildings may be mentioned as worthy of attention, — the great wholesale and retail dry-goods establishment of Jordan, Marsh, & Co. ; the marble building on the right occupied by Macullar, Williams, & Parker's clothing store; the Old South Church ; the Transcript, Journal, and Globe offices, — all on the same side ; and on the left the Old Corner Bookstore at the corner of School Street,

See " *Boston Illustrated*," *a pictorial handbook of Boston.*

and several other much more recent and elegant buildings. We pass through Cornhill, with the extensive printing-house of Rand, Avery, & Co., and the numerous book and stationery stores, to Scollay Square, whence we set out. The walk thus sketched is probably not more than two miles in length.

The Back Bay and the Common.

We will next sketch a tour of the Back-bay region. The starting-point is Park-street Church, where we will take a Beacon-street car. We pass through Tremont, Boylston, Clarendon, and Marlborough Streets to Dartmouth. Here we are in the region which is now rapidly filling up with elegant dwelling-houses. We leave the car, and pass into Beacon Street, through which we walk to Berkeley Street, between some of the finest mansions in Boston. We walk through Berkeley Street, passing by, first, the very beautiful First Church (Unitarian), then the costly and imposing Central Church (Cong. Trin.). Between the two is Commonwealth Avenue, already a fine street, but one that will be still more delightful when it has been extended, as is designed, to Brookline, and when the rows of trees shall have attained greater size. We pass also, beyond, the Central Church, and the fine building of the Boston Society of Natural History, which is open to the public every Wednesday and Saturday. We must turn down Boylston Street to see its companion building, the Massachusetts Institute of Technology. Retracing our steps, we pass up Boylston Street to Arlington, where we turn to the left, and walk on the Public-garden side of the street, the better to see the Arlington-street Church and the magnificent residences on the westerly side, to the central gate of the Garden. On entering, we find ourselves facing Ball's most excellent equestrian statue of Washington. To the

Engravings and Descriptions in "Boston Illustrated."

left we see a group of statuary representing the Good
Samaritan, on a pedestal, — the noble gift of a private
citizen, to adorn these grounds, and to commemorate the
discovery of anæsthetics. Beyond, at the centre of the
northerly side, we see the statue of Edward Everett. We
cross the bridge, and pass directly through the Garden, unless we prefer to wander about, or to rest upon
one of the seats so abundantly provided ; and, crossing
Charles Street, we are in the Common. Here is occupation for many a leisure hour. We may enjoy the specta-
cle of the boys at their sport on the Parade Ground ; we
may wander up to the Boylston-street side, and look into
the ancient graveyard or the pleasant deer-park ; we may
climb the hill, and see the foundation of the Soldiers'
Monument; we may sit down by the Frog Pond, and
watch the boys and girls at play; we may go and see
the famous Old Elm, which has been a living tree since
Boston was first settled, and from whose branches more
than one supposed witch has been suspended ; or we may
walk idly along the broad malls in the refreshing shade
of the grand old trees. We should not fail, however, to
see, before our return to Park-street Church, the fine
bronze fountain near the Park-street mall, which the gene-
rosity of a single citizen has placed there. Nor could
the tour end more profitably than by a visit to the State
House, where scores of interesting objects are to be seen,
and by climbing to the cupola, from which the best view of
Boston is to be had.

The South End.

Our next trip is one that can be made mostly by
horse-cars, and calls for but a small exercise of pedes-
trian powers. We will start, as before, from Park-street
Church, taking a Lenox-street car, and riding to its
southern terminus. We pass over familiar ground to

See "*Boston Illustrated,*" *a pictorial handbook of Boston.*

Boylston Street, but continue in Tremont Street to the South End. After crossing the bridge over the Boston and Albany Railroad, we pass, on the right, the extensive Bay-State Moulding Mills. Beyond Berkeley Street, on the corner of which is the elegant new Odd Fellows' Hall, we come into the region of churches. On the right is the Clarendon-street Baptist Church, close by the Smith American Organ Factory. On the left are the peculiar-shaped brick tower of the Shawmut Congregational Church, and the beautiful structure of the Tremont-street Methodist Society. Arrived at the end of our route, we notice the immense factory where Chickering's pianofortes are made. We pass through Northampton Street northward to Columbus Avenue, merely to glance at that fine thoroughfare, from the extreme end of which we see the steeple of Park-street Church, and to pass up one block to West Chester Park. We walk through the latter avenue and Chester Square to Washington Street. One block northward on Washington Street brings us to the marble-front Commonwealth Hotel. Another block, and we come to Worcester Square, on the right-hand side. We pass through Worcester Square to Harrison Avenue, having in front of us the immense City Hospital. Turning down Harrison Avenue, we come, at Concord Street, to the Church of the Immaculate Conception, and Boston College. At Newton Street we turn once more towards Washington Street, but pass into Franklin Square, in order the better to examine the imposing front of the St. James Hotel. On the opposite side of Washington Street is the mate to Franklin Square, — Blackstone Square. A short distance down Washington Street we come to the yet unfinished but majestic Cathedral of the Holy Cross. On the left, and a little farther on, is the Continental Hotel, — an immense and very elegant marble-front hotel on the French flat-system. We may now take any horse-car that

Engravings and Descriptions in "Boston Illustrated."

overtakes us, and it will carry us back to our point of
starting. There are several interesting objects to be
noticed on the way ; but they need not be specified here.

South Boston.

There are several public buildings in **South Boston**
that should be visited if time permit. We may take a
car marked "South Boston, Broadway," at Scollay
Square, and pass at first through a district we have
already visited. In Summer Street we see many fine
business houses that we have not previously included in
our trips, and we also pass the fine stone church of
Trinity parish (Episcopal), of which the Rev. Phillips
Brooks, one of the most popular clergymen in Boston, is
pastor and rector. In Chauncy Street we see many large
dry-goods houses, and pass, on the right, the fine building
of the Massachusetts Charitable Mechanic Association,
which is occupied by the Boston and the National
Boards of Trade. On our route we pass by the United
States Hotel, and the stations of the Albany and the Old
Colony Railroads. We are supposed to have provided
ourselves at the head-quarters of the Institution for the
Blind, No. 20 Bromfield Street, with permits to enter that
asylum; and we soon arrive on the Heights where it is
situated. The visit cannot fail to be exceedingly interesting. After leaving the Institution, we walk through
Broadway and M Streets, by Independence Square, to
the territory occupied by the House of Correction, House
of Industry, Insane Hospital, and Almshouse. Returning to the corner of K Street and Broadway, we take a
Bay-View and Eighth-street car into the city by another
route.

East Boston.

The principal objects of interest in East Boston are
the Grand-Junction Wharves and the Cunard Steamer

Docks. We start once more from Scollay Square by an East-Boston car, and pass through the poorest quarter of the city, — the Five Points of Boston. After a pleasant trip across the ferry, we are landed very near the Grand-Junction Wharves, which we reach by passing through Marginal Street. Cunard Wharf lies directly on the way, and we shall be peculiarly unfortunate if we do not see one of the great ocean freight steamers at the dock or lying in the stream. The scene on the arrival of one of these steamers, when she is discharging her cargo or reloading, is full of interest; and the busy activity of the Grand-Junction Wharves at all times makes this one of the trips that ought to be taken.

SUBURBAN TRIPS.

Charlestown.

We will make the circuit of the suburban towns, beginning on the North. Charlestown is reached by any car of the Middlesex Railroad ; but we will take a Chelsea car, of the Lynn and Boston Railroad, that will carry us by the Navy Yard. On our way we pass by the Boston and Maine Railroad Station in Haymarket Square, and over Charles-River Bridge into Charlestown Square, where we shall see the fine hotel known as the Waverley, which was built out of the profits of the " Waverley Magazine." Arrived at the Navy Yard, we leave the car, and examine the numerous points of interest within. On leaving the Yard, we shall see the tall shaft of Bunker-Hill Monument, and shall need no guide to direct us to it. We must of course climb the monument, and obtain one of the finest views to be had anywhere. From the south window we have a complete bird's-eye view of Boston ; from the east, the harbor ; from the north, Everett, Chelsea,

Engraving and Description in "Boston Illustrated."

Revere, Malden, and Lynn ; and from the west window we look out to Cambridge and Arlington, to Watertown and Belmont; and in a clear day we may see Wachusett Mountain in Worcester County, and Kearsarge and the White Mountains in New Hampshire. The several points to be noticed are briefly described elsewhere. From the monument, we should pass near enough to the State Prison at least to see its gloomy and forbidding walls; and a walk into the city from that point will not be a great task. If after crossing by the lower or Charles-River Bridge, we pass down Commercial Street a short distance, we shall be in the immediate vicinity of the ancient Copp's-Hill Burying Ground, between Snowhill and Hull Streets : that will well repay a visit. We then pass through Hull Street to Salem Street, by Christ Church, — the oldest church-building yet remaining in the city. From Salem Street we pass into Hanover, and through that formerly narrow but now spacious street, past the American House, — the largest hotel in the city, — on the right, into Court Street and Scollay Square, whence we started.

Cambridge.

In order to see as much as possible of Cambridge in one trip, we will take at Bowdoin Square, opposite the Revere House, a car marked "East Cambridge, Harvard Square." We pass through Green and Leverett Streets, and cross Craigie's Bridge. In East Cambridge we see a large number of important factories. We pass through Cambridge Street, its whole length, to Harvard Square, where we alight, and inspect the old and new buildings of Harvard College. In coming to the square through Cambridge Street, we have passed, first, Appleton Chapel, in the corner of the college yard, then Holworthy Hall, built with money raised by a lottery, Stoughton, Hollis, and Harvard, — all dormitories. We

See "Boston Illustrated," a pictorial handbook of Boston.

now see close to the fence old Massachusetts Hall, built in the seventeenth century, the oldest building in the yard, having a clock-face that was put up in 1725. In the corner nearest to Brattle Street is Gray Hall; and a little beyond, on Harvard Street, is Boylston Hall, where is deposited the College Museum: that may be visited. Boylston Hall may be recognized from its being the only rough-granite building in the yard. A short distance beyond, and farther removed from the street, is Gore Hall, where is the rich old library of the University, — a building which is also open to the public. The buildings of the Lawrence Scientific School, the Divinity School, the Museum of Comparative Zoölogy, and the Memorial Hall, are outside the College yard, between Cambridge and Kirkland Streets, and beyond Kirkland Street. After having inspected these several buildings, we take a Garden-street and Mount-Auburn car. We pass by the Common on the right, and by the elegant new church of the Shepard Congregational Society on the left. In the middle of the street is the famous Washington Elm, under which Gen. Washington took command of the American army in 1775. At Mount Auburn we pass into that great city of the dead, where again we shall find occupation for all the time that can be spared. No one should fail to visit the chapel, and to ascend to the top of the tower. In returning, we take a Mount-Auburn car that is not marked "Garden Street," and we shall then return through Brattle Street to Harvard Square. On our way we pass by the residence of the poet Longfellow, — an old mansion of the Revolutionary period, used in 1775 by Gen. Washington as his head-quarters. On our way into the city through Main Street, we see a great many fine residences and churches; and from West-Boston Bridge we get another excellent view of Boston, especially the Back-bay region. It will be well to finish up our views in Boston proper, by leaving the car at Charles Street, just

---

Engraving and Description in "Boston Illustrated."

after crossing the bridge, and turning to the left near the Mason & Hamlin Cabinet Organ Factory, we shall soon come to the city jail, a fine granite building. A little farther on we see the magnificent building of the Massachusetts General Hospital : we pass up Allen Street, and then, turning to the right, pass through Chambers to Cambridge Street. Ascending Cambridge Street, we see on the left the old building of the West Church. Nearly opposite is Temple Street, up which we walk, past Grace Church on the right, to the massive stone Beacon-hill reservoir. This solid structure now stands where was the highest point of Beacon Hill before it was cut down. We go over the hill, and through Mount-Vernon Street to Beacon Street. Turning to the left, we soon reach the Boston Athenæum, where is a fine gallery of paintings on exhibition, and a very large library, which may be visited. On leaving the Athenæum, we pass through Beacon and Somerset Streets and Pemberton Square, — a nest of lawyers', architects', and corporation offices, — to Scollay Square.

Chestnut Hill.

We follow our plan of describing routes to be taken by those who wish to see the leading points of interest in and about Boston without incurring the expense of a private carriage. Nevertheless, it must be said that the drive to Chestnut Hill is one of the most charming imaginable ; and if one drive, and one only, is to be taken by the visitor to Boston, this should certainly be chosen in preference to all others. The cheaper conveyance, however, is by the steam-cars. A train of the Boston, Hartford, and Erie Railroad should be taken at the Boston and Albany Station, and a ticket purchased for Chestnut Hill. The train will stop at several points of interest along the way ; but these need not be described. Nor need any thing be said of the most lovely views at Chest-

See "*Boston Illustrated*," *a pictorial handbook of Boston.*

nut Hill itself. If the visitor has driven to the Reservoir, he will find numerous ways of returning to the city different from that by which he went out; but the less extravagant traveller must return by the railroad.

Roxbury and Dorchester.

The horse-car routes through these new wards of Boston are so arranged, and the objects of interest are so far distant from each other, that, if one wishes simply to see the sights of Boston, he must occupy a great deal of time. We shall therefore in this place merely indicate the routes to be taken to each particular point, leaving each one to decide which of them, if not all, he will see. Forest-hills Cemetery is reached by the Forest-hills horse-cars, which start from Park-street Church. The cemetery lies in the town of West Roxbury, and in reaching it we pass through an interesting part of Roxbury. If we take a Dorchester and Grove-hall car, also from Park-street Church, we shall pass, on Warren Street, in Roxbury, the estate of Gen. Joseph Warren, who fell at Bunker Hill; and, after noticing on either side the elegant estates and fine residences which line Warren Street, we come to Grove Hall, now occupied for a Consumptives' Home. The Mount-Pleasant cars will carry us to a beautiful part of Roxbury; and near the terminus of the line is the estate of Gov. Eustis, with its ample grounds and spacious residence. Dorchester is very beautiful in many parts; and the horse-cars, which start from the foot of Summer Street, or the Old Colony and the Hartford and Erie Railroads will carry one to almost any desired point.

The Harbor.

A visit to Boston should not be considered as finished before one has taken a sail down the harbor. There are several routes that may be followed; and it would be difficult to choose among them, since they all afford an opportunity to see nearly every point of interest in this part of the suburbs. They all take one past the forts and among the islands, give a view of the surrounding country, and whether running to Hull, to Nantasket Beach, to Hingham, or to Nahant, reach some point that will, by its beauty and the interest that attaches to it, well repay a visit.

A Sight from Bunker-Hill Monument.

It is so difficult to identify familiar objects from a new point of view, that it is well to have some assistance in looking over such a vast expanse of country as is opened to our view from the top of Bunker-hill Monument. We will suppose the visitor to the monument to look out first to the north. We notice, first, the singular peninsula of Nahant, with its long neck reaching to Lynn, the city of shoes; and then we follow the coast across the mouth of Saugus River, along Revere or Chelsea Beach, to the little town of Winthrop. To the left of the coast, we see the city of Chelsea spread out before us. The towns of Malden, Everett, Melrose, and Saugus, with their numerous villages, and the trains on the Eastern and the Boston and Maine Roads passing along their swift but apparently snail-like course.

We turn now to the west, and here a glorious prospect opens before us. The entire country is dotted with villages, crossed by railroads, watered by rivers, made beautiful by being covered with pretty and comfortable dwelling-houses. On the extreme right, we see close beneath our feet the new city of Somerville; and Medford lies beyond it. Turning a little to the left, we look out over Arlington and towards Lexington; and, if it be a clear day, we may see the White Mountains from this

See "Boston Illustrated," a pictorial handbook of Boston.

point: while due west we see Cambridge, the University, the United States Arsenal in Watertown, and Mount Auburn.

A little farther south we see Brighton and its stock-yards; the beautiful town of Newton,— formerly a cluster of pretty villages, but rapidly becoming an area wholly covered by one great village; Brookline, with its reservoir; beyond, the Chestnut-hill Reservoir; and a little more to the south, Jamaica Pond.

Once more we change our position, and look out of the south window upon Boston. The sight is at first somewhat confusing. We see a vast area completely covered with dwellings, churches, and warehouses. Only the practised eye can pick out any particular building that differs but slightly from the rest in architecture. We shall have no difficulty in finding the State House. Close to it is the First Baptist Church on Somerset Street. We can see the peculiar steeple of the Old South to the left; and the churches on the Back Bay may be easily distinguished. From this station we may see the line of every railroad out of Boston. Roxbury and Dorchester, now constituting four of the wards of Boston, lie beyond the city proper; and at the extreme left we may see, on Dorchester Heights in South Boston, the Perkins Institution for the Blind, and beyond, several city institutions which are only pleasant objects to look at when visited voluntarily.

We look out now from the east window upon the harbor and East Boston. Forts Winthrop and Independence lie comparatively near, and will easily be distinguished. Upon Long-Island Head we see the lighthouse that has been erected to guide vessels into the inner harbor. Farther down the harbor is the famous Fort Warren, and beyond it the town of Hull. If the weather is clear, we may see, at the entrance of the harbor, the outer Boston Light. Nearly beneath our eyes lies East

Boston; and we may easily distinguish the extensive wharves and grain elevator of the Boston and Albany Railroad, and the wharf where the Cunard steamers land their passengers and cargo.

A SERIES OF DRIVES.

To Chelsea Beach.

An interesting drive for visitors from the interior, to whom the sight of the sea is a novelty, may be laid out as follows: starting from any central point, — as, for instance, Scollay Square, — we will proceed through Hanover, Union, and Charlestown Streets, over Charlesriver Bridge, to Charlestown. We then pay a visit to Bunker-hill Monument and the Navy Yard on our way, and proceed over Chelsea Bridge to Chelsea; thence directly through the city to Revere Village, where we turn to the right, and ride down to Revere or Chelsea Beach. This is a magnificent beach, smooth and hard, upon which the waves dash grandly. In returning, we may come back by way of Everett, Malden, Medford, and the new city of Somerville, seeing how rapidly the suburbs of Boston are growing, and entering the city by way of Craigie's Bridge, through East Cambridge.

To Lexington, Watertown, and Mount Auburn.

The easiest way to visit the battle-ground of Lexington is by railroad; still, it may be reached by a rather long but very interesting drive. We pass out of Boston by the West-Boston (Cambridge) Bridge, and, taking Broadway, follow the direct road though Cambridge, past Fresh Pond, into and through Arlington into Lex-

See " *Boston Illustrated,*" *a pictorial handbook of Boston.*

ington. Turning then to the north, we ride through East-Lexington Village to Lexington Village and the battle-field. On our return, we visit Waltham, where the great American Watch Factory is situated, and, passing through Newton into Watertown, stop to look over the United States Arsenal; thence to Mount Auburn, by the houses of Lowell and Longfellow, and the Washington Elm, to Harvard Square and the buildings of the University, elsewhere described, and thence back to Boston.

To Chestnut Hill and Newton.

This is the favorite direction for drives out of Boston. The route is by way of Beacon Street, through the whole length of that magnificent avenue, and over the Mill-dam road. On reaching the fork in the road, we take the branch to the right,—Brighton Avenue,—and continue to the Baptist Church at the corner of Cambridge Street. We have been passing over the "Brighton road," famed in song, and the popular sleigh-drive on the few occasions in winter when that class of vehicles can be brought into use. We turn now to the left, and pass through Brighton to Newton Corner, thence by Centre Street to Newton Centre, where we take Beacon Street, and return by way of the Chestnut-hill Reservoir, and from thence in a straight line, by Corey's Hill, into Boston by the way we went out.

To Jamaica Plain and Forest Hills.

Our next drive is to the suburbs on the south of the city; and, as before, we will make a circuit. Passing once more out of the city by Beacon Street and the Mill-dam road, we take the left branch, and pass, through Western Avenue and the beautiful village of Longwood, to the Brookline reservoir on Boylston Street. From the reservoir, by a winding road that gives us some glimpses of lovely scenery, we come to the charming Jamaica Pond, around which we ride ; thence to Forest-hills cemetery, and back into Boston by way of Shawmut Avenue, Egleston Square, Walnut Avenue, Warren Street, and Washington Street.

To Dorchester.

Our last suburban drive takes us through the greater part of Roxbury and Dorchester. We ride, through Tremont Street and Shawmut Avenue, to Dudley Street, then through Warren Street, past the Warren House, to Grove Hall, and by way of Blue-Hill Avenue to Mattapan Village and the Blue Hills in Milton. Returning, we ride through Milton Lower Mills, Harrison Square, Savin Hill, and South Boston, passing by the Blind Asylum if we wish, over the Federal-street Bridge into the city.

Conveyances about Boston.

HORSE-RAILROADS.

Metropolitan Railroad.

This company serves all the North, West, and South Ends of Boston, Brookline, West Roxbury, Roxbury, a part of Dorchester, a part of South Boston, and East Boston. It has a large number of routes, which are in detail as follows : —

Boston Neck and Dépôt Cars. — Inward trips, from the corner of Washington and Camden Streets, through

Washington, Temple Place, Tremont, Court, Green, Leverett, and Causeway Streets, to the Fitchburg-railroad Station. Outward **trips**, from Fitchburg-railroad Station, through Causeway, Portland, Chardon, Court, Cornhill, Washington, Summer, Chauncy, Harrison Avenue, East-Dover, and Washington Streets, to corner of Camden.

Boston Neck and Charles-Street Cars. — Inward **trips**, from corner of Washington and Camden Streets, through Washington, Temple Place, Tremont, Court, Green, Chambers, Cambridge, and Charles Streets, to Beacon Street. Outward trips, back through Charles, Cambridge, Court, Cornhill, Washington, Summer, Chauncy, Harrison Avenue, East-Dover, and Washington Streets, to Camden Street.

Boston Neck and Chelsea-Ferry Cars. — Inward trips, from corner of Camden and Washington Streets by route of the dépôt cars to corner of Court and Hanover Streets, thence through Hanover Street to Chelsea Ferry. Outward trips, through Hanover Street to Court, and thence outward by route of the dépôt Cars.

Mount-Pleasant Cars. — Inward trips, from Stoughton Street, Dorchester, near Roxbury line, through Stoughton, Dudley, Dearborn, Eustis, Washington, Temple Place, and Tremont Streets, to Tremont House. Outward trips, from Tremont House, back, through Tremont, West-Dover, Washington, Eustis, Dearborn, Dudley, and Stoughton Streets, to station.

Warren-Street Cars. — Inward trips, from corner of Warren and Moreland Streets, through Warren, Washington, Temple Place, and Tremont Streets, to Tremont House. Outward trips, back, through Tremont, West-Dover, Washington, and Warren Streets, to station.

Grove-Hall Cars. — From Grove Hall, junction of Warren Street and Blue-Hill Avenue, through Warren Street, and thence by route of Warren-street cars, to

---

Engravings and Descriptions in "Boston Illustrated."

Tremont House. Outward trips, from Tremont House by route of Warren-street cars extended to Grove Hall.

Dorchester and Grove-Hall Cars. — From Washington Street, Dorchester, near Town Hall, through Washington and Warren Streets, and thence to Tremont House by route of Warren-street cars. Outward trips, by route of Warren-street cars, extended by inward route of Dorchester cars to station.

Norfolk-House Cars. — Round trips, starting from Norfolk House, Eliot Square, through Dudley, Washington, Temple Place, Tremont, Cornhill, Washington, Summer, Chauncy, Harrison Avenue, East-Dover, and Washington Streets, to Eliot Square. The inward trip extends to the Old-South Church : the outward trip begins at Park-street Church.

Egleston-Square Cars. — Inward trips, from corner of Egleston Square and Shawmut Avenue, through Shawmut Avenue, Washington, Temple Place, and Tremont Streets, to Tremont House. Outward trips, from Tremont House back, through Tremont, West-Dover, and Washington Streets, and Shawmut Avenue, to Egleston Square.

Forest-Hills Cars. — Inward trips, from Forest-hills Station, through Shawmut Avenue, and the route of Egleston-square cars, to the Tremont House. Outward trips, by route of Egleston-square cars extended to Forest-hills Station.

Lenox-Street Cars. — Inward trips, from corner of Tremont and Lenox Streets through Tremont Street to the Tremont House. Outward trips, back, through Tremont Street, to Lenox Street.

Lenox-Street and Dépôt Cars. — Inward trips, from corner of Lenox and Tremont Streets, through Tremont, Berkeley, Boylston, Tremont, Court, Green, Leverett, and Causeway Streets, to Fitchburg-railroad Station. Outward trips, back, through Causeway, Portland, Char-

See "*Boston Illustrated,*" *a pictorial handbook of Boston.*

don, Court, Cornhill, Washington, Temple Place, Boylston, Berkeley, and Tremont Streets, to Lenox Street.

Tremont-Street Cars. — Inward trips, from crossing of Tremont Street and Providence Railroad, through Tremont Street, to Tremont House. Outward trips, back, through Tremont Street, to Station.

Jamaica-Plain (*West-Roxbury*) *Cars.* — Inward trips, from Jamaica Plain, through Austin, Centre, Pynchon, and Tremont Streets, to the Tremont House. Outward trips, back over the same route.

Brookline Cars. — Inward trips, from Harvard Square, Brookline, through Washington Street (Brookline) and Tremont Street, to Tremont House. Outward trips, back over the same route.

Providence-Depôt Cars. — Inward trips, from Park Square, through Boylston and Tremont Streets, to the Tremont House. Outward trips, back over the same route.

Beacon-Street Cars. — Round trips, from corner of Gloucester and Marlboro' Streets, through Marlboro', Clarendon, Boylston, Tremont, Cornhill, Washington, Temple Place, Tremont, Boylston, Clarendon, and Marlboro' Streets, to Gloucester Street.

East-Boston Cars. — Inward trips, from East-Boston and Chelsea (Meridian-street) Bridge, through Meridian Street, Maverick Square, and Sumner Street, to the ferry, over the ferry to Lincoln's Wharf, through Battery, Hanover, Court, Cornhill, Washington, Temple Place, and Tremont Streets, to Tremont House. Outward trips continue through Tremont, Court, Hanover, and Battery Streets, and by the ferry over the inward route.

Mount Bowdoin and Meeting-House-Hill Cars. — Inward trips, from corner of Washington and Bowdoin Streets, (Dorchester), through Bowdoin, Hancock, Boston, Dorchester, and Federal Streets, to foot of Summer Street, Boston. Outward trips, back over the same route.

Field's-Corner Cars. — Inward trips, from crossing of Adams and Hancock Streets with Dorchester Avenue (Dorchester), through Dorchester Avenue and Federal Street, to foot of Summer Street. Outward trips, back over the same route.

Milton Cars. — Inward trips, from corner of Washington and Adams Streets and Dorchester Avenue, Milton Village, Dorchester, through Dorchester Avenue and Federal Street, to foot of Summer Street. Outward trips, back over the same route.

South-Boston Railroad.

South-Boston Cars. — Inward trips, from the office of the company, corner of K Street and Broadway, through Broadway, Emerson, Third, Dorchester, Broadway, Federal, Kneeland, South, Beach, Washington, Boylston, and Tremont Streets, to Scollay Square. Outward trips, from Scollay Square, through Cornhill, Washington, Summer, Chauncy, Harrison Avenue, Beach, Federal, Broadway, Dorchester, Third, Emerson, and Broadway, to office of the company.

Broadway Cars. — Inward trips, from office of company, through Broadway to Federal, thence into Boston proper by the route of the South-Boston line. Outward trips, from Scollay Square, by route of South-Boston cars to Broadway, thence through Broadway to the station.

City-Point Cars. — Inward trips, from City Point, through Fourth, L, and Emerson Streets, and the route of the South-Boston cars, into Boston proper. Outward trips, from Scollay Square, by route of the South-Boston cars, thence, by Broadway, L, and Fourth Streets, to City Point.

Bay-View and Eighth-Street Cars. — Inward trips, from

corner of K and Broadway, through K, Eighth, E, Sixth, C, Fourth, and Federal, to Kneeland, thence inward, by the route of the South-Boston cars. Outward trips, from Scollay Square, by the route of the South-Boston cars, to Federal, thence, by inward route of the Bay-View cars, to the office of the company.

Union Railway.

This company's cars run to all parts of Cambridge, and to Watertown, Brighton, Arlington, and Somerville. It has nearly twenty routes, which are in detail as follows. To save repetitions, it may be remarked, that outside of Boston the inward and outward routes are the same, and that the starting-point of all the cars in Boston is Bowdoin Square.

Prospect-Street (Cambridgeport) Cars. — Inward trips, from corner of Prospect and Main Streets, Cambridge, through Main Street, West-Boston Bridge, and Cambridge Street, to Bowdoin Square. Outward trips, through Green, Chambers, and Cambridge Streets, West-Boston Bridge and Main Street, to the station.

Riverside-Press Cars. — Inward trips, from Riverside Press, foot of River Street, through River and Main Streets, West-Boston Bridge, and Cambridge Street, to Bowdoin Square. Outward trips, through Green, Chambers, and Cambridge Streets, West-Boston Bridge, Main, and River Streets, to station.

Brighton Cars. — Inward trips, from Brighton village, through Cambridge Street (Brighton), River, and Main Streets, West-Boston Bridge, and Cambridge Street, to Bowdoin Square. Outward trips, through Green, Chambers, and Cambridge Streets, West-Boston Bridge, and thence by inward route.

Newton-Corner Cars. — Inward trips, from Boston and Albany railroad station (Newton Corner), through Brigh-

---

Engravings and Descriptions in "Boston Illustrated."

ton Village, River and Main Streets (Cambridge), West-Boston Bridge, and Cambridge Street, to Bowdoin Square. Outward trips, through Green, Chambers, and Cambridge Streets, and thence by inward route.

Harvard-Square Cars. — Inward trips, from Harvard Square (Cambridge), through Harvard and Main Streets, West-Boston Bridge and Cambridge Street, to Bowdoin Square. Outward trips, through Green, Chambers, and Cambridge Streets, and thence by inward route.

Mount-Auburn (Garden-Street) Cars. — From Mount Auburn, near the railroad station, through Brattle Street, Concord Avenue, Garden Street, North Avenue, Harvard Square, Harvard and Main Streets, West-Boston Bridge, and Cambridge Street, to Bowdoin Square. Outward trips, through Green, Chambers, and Cambridge Streets, and thence by inward route.

Mount-Auburn Cars. — Inward trips, from Mount Auburn, (same station), through Brattle Street to Harvard Square, thence into Boston by route of Harvard-square line. Outward trips, through Green, Chambers, and Cambridge Streets, and thence by inward route.

Watertown Cars. — Inward trips, from Watertown Village, through Pleasant, Mount-Auburn, and Brattle Streets to Harvard Square, thence into Boston by route of Harvard-square line. Outward trips, through Green, Chambers, and Cambridge Streets, and thence by inward route.

North-Avenue (Rice-Street) Cars. — Inward trips, from corner of Rice Street and North Avenue, through North Avenue, to Harvard Square, thence into Boston by route of the Harvard-Square line. Outward trips, through Green, Chambers, and Cambridge Streets, and thence by inward route.

North-Avenue Cars. — From corner of North Avenue and Chester Streets, through North Avenue to Harvard Square, thence into Boston by route of the Harvard-

See "Boston Illustrated," a pictorial handbook of Boston.

square line. Outward trips, through Green, Chambers, and Cambridge Streets, and thence by inward route.

Arlington Cars. — Inward trips, from Arlington Village, through Arlington and **North** Avenue to Harvard Square, thence into Boston by route of Harvard-square line. Outward trips, through **Green,** Chambers, and Cambridge Streets, and thence by inward route.

Broadway (Inman-Street) Cars. — Inward trips, from **corner of** Broadway and Inman Streets (Cambridge), **through** Broadway, West-Boston Bridge, and Cambridge Street, to Bowdoin Square. Outward trips, through Green, Chambers, and Cambridge Streets, West-Boston Bridge, and Broadway, to corner of Inman Street.

Broadway (Harvard-Square) Cars. — Inward trips, from Harvard Square, through Harvard Square, Cambridge Street, Broadway, **West-Boston Bridge,** and Cambridge **Street, to Bowdoin S**quare. Outward trips, through Green, Chambers, and Cambridge Streets, West-Boston Bridge, and Broadway, to Harvard Square.

Eighth-Street (East Cambridge) Cars. — Inward trips, from corner of Eighth and Cambridge Streets, East Cambridge, through Cambridge and **Bridge** Streets, Craigie's Bridge, Leverett, Minot, Lowell, Causeway, Portland, and Chardon Streets, **to** Bowdoin Square. Outward trips, through Green **and** Leverett Streets, Craigie's Bridge, Bridge, and Cambridge Streets, to station.

Atwood's-Crossing (East Cambridge) Cars. — **Inward trips, from** corner of Beacon, Hampshire, and Cambridge Streets, through Cambridge and Bridge Streets, Craigie's **Bridge,** and thence to Bowdoin Square by route of Eighth-street **cars.** Outward trips, through Green and Leverett Streets, Craigie's **Bridge,** and thence by inward route.

East-Cambridge (Harvard-Square) Cars. — Inward trips, from Harvard Square, through Harvard Square, Cambridge, and Bridge Streets, and thence to Bowdoin Square by route of the Eighth-street cars. Outward trips, through Green and Leverett Streets, Craigie's Bridge, and thence by inward route.

Union-Square (Somerville) Cars. — Inward trips, from Union Square, Somerville, though Milk Street, Somerville, Bridge Street, East Cambridge, and thence to Bowdoin Square, by route of the Eighth-street cars. Outward trips, through Green and Leverett Streets, Craigie's Bridge, and thence by inward route.

Somerville Cars. — Inward trips, from the company's stable at North Cambridge, through Elm and Milk Streets (Somerville), Bridge Street (East Cambridge), and thence to Bowdoin Square by route of the Eighth-street cars. Outward trips, through Green and Leverett Streets, Craigie's Bridge, and thence by inward route.

Middlesex Railroad.

The cars of this line run to Charlestown, Somerville, Malden, Everett, and Medford. The routes of the several lines are given below in detail.

Charlestown-Neck Cars. — Inward trips, from Somerville line on Main Street (Charlestown), through Main Street, over Warren Bridge, through Beverly Street, Haymarket Square, Sudbury and Court Streets, to Scollay Square. Outward trips, from Scollay Square, through Cornhill, Washington Street, Dock Square, Union Street, Haymarket Square, Charlestown Street, over Charles-river Bridge, through Charlestown Square, Warren and Main Streets, to Somerville line.

Bunker-Hill Cars. — Inward trips, from station, near summit of Bunker-hill Street, through Bunker-hill, Vine, and Chelsea Streets, Charlestown Square, thence into Boston by same route as Neck cars. Outward trips, from Scollay Square, same route as Neck cars, to Charles-

---

See "Boston Illustrated," a pictorial handbook of Boston.

town Square, thence through Warren, Henley, Chelsea, Vine, and Bunker-hill Streets, to the station.

Malden and Everett Cars. — Inward trips, from Malden Centre, through Main, Chelsea, School, and Charlestown Streets, over Malden Bridge, thence into Boston by same route as the Neck cars. Outward trips, from Scollay Square by route of the Neck cars to the terminus of that line, thence to **Malden** Centre by the **inward route.**

Winter-Hill Cars. — Inward trips, from Winter Hill, in Somerville, through Broadway, to starting-point of the Neck cars, thence into Boston by the Neck route. Outward trips, from Scollay Square by **the Neck route to** the Somerville line, thence by Broadway (Somerville) to Winter Hill.

Medford Cars. — Inward trips, from Salem (opposite Ashland) Street, in Medford, to Winter Hill, thence into Boston by route of the Winter-hill and Neck cars. Outward trips, from Scollay Square, by Neck and Winter-hill routes, to Winter Hill, thence by inward **route to** station.

Union-Square Cars. — Inward trips, from Union Square (Somerville), through Milk and Washington Streets, to Main Street (Charlestown) thence into Boston by route of the Neck cars. Outward trips, from Scollay Square by route of Neck cars, and inward **route of** Union-square cars to the station.

Lynn and Boston Railroad.

Chelsea Cars. — Inward trips, from Washington Avenue (Prattsville), Chelsea, through Washington Avenue, Broadway, Chelsea Bridge, Chelsea Street, Charlestown Square, Warren Bridge, Beverly, and Charlestown Streets, Haymarket Square, Sudbury and Court Streets, to Scollay Square. Outward trips, through Cornhill, Dock Square, Union Street, Haymarket Square,

Charlestown Street, Charles-river Bridge, Charlestown Square, Park, Henley, and Chelsea Streets, Chelsea Bridge, Broadway, and Washington Avenue, to the station.

Revere Cars. — Inward trips, from Revere over the Salem turnpike to Broadway in Chelsea, thence into Boston by route of the Chelsea cars. Outward trips, from Scollay Square by the route of the Chelsea cars to Broadway, thence by inward route of Revere cars to station.

Chelsea (Revere) Beach Cars. — From Revere Beach to the Salem turnpike, thence by route of Revere cars into Boston. Outward trips, from Scollay Square by route of Revere cars, and inward route of Chelsea-beach cars, to the beach in Revere.

Lynn and Swampscott Cars. — Inward trips, from Lewis Street (Lynn), through Broad, Market, South, and Common Streets, and Western Avenue, thence over Salem turnpike, through Saugus and Revere, and by route of the Revere cars, into Boston. Outward trips, from Scollay Square by route of Chelsea and Revere cars, and inward route of Lynn cars, to Lewis Street, Lynn.

Citizen's Omnibus Line.

From Charlestown to Boston, from foot of Salem Street (Charlestown), over Warren Bridge, through Causeway, Leverett, Green, Court, and Washington Streets, to Concord Street. From Boston to Charlestown, back over the same route.

Hack Fares.

The following rates of fare have been established by the Board of Aldermen for all public hacks and carriages. Any driver who asks or receives more is subject to fine,

---

See " *Boston Illustrated,*" a pictorial handbook of Boston.

and the forfeiture of license; and like penalties are in-
flicted for refusing to carry a passenger from any railroad-
station or steamboat-landing to any part of the city.

Within the city proper, fifty cents for each passenger;
but a driver may charge one dollar for carrying one
person from points north of Cambridge, Court, and State
Streets, to points south of Dover, or west of Berkeley
Streets. For more than one passenger, the charge is fifty
cents each.

From one place to another in East Boston, from one
place to another in South Boston, or from one place to
another in Roxbury, the charge is fifty cents for each
passenger.

Fares to Roxbury. For one passenger from a point
north of Essex and Boylston Streets to any point in
Roxbury, $2.50; the same for two persons; $3.00 for
three persons; $3.00 for four persons.

For one passenger from points south of Essex and **Boylston,** but north of Dover and Berkeley, $2.00; the same
amount for two persons; for three persons, $2.25; for
four persons, $2.50. From points south of Dover and
Berkeley Streets to any part of Roxbury, $1.25; for two
persons, 75 cents each; for three or more persons, 50 cents
each.

For one passenger between any part of the city proper
and either South or East Boston, $1.00; for two or more
persons, 75 cents each.

For one passenger from one point to another in Dorchester, $1.00; for each additional passenger, 50 cents.
The rates of fare between Dorchester and the other parts
of the city are complicated; but they will be found posted
in every public carriage in the city.

Hackmen are not allowed to charge any thing extra for
baggage carried. In Dorchester, however, they are
allowed to charge 50 cents for each additional trunk
above two carried by one person. Children under four

Engravings and Descriptions in "Boston Illustrated."

years of age are carried free; between four and twelve, half-rates only are allowed. Additional charges are permitted between midnight and six o'clock in the morning, according to definite rules, which every passenger may read for himself, as posted in the carriage.

Ferries to East Boston and Chelsea.

North Ferry. — From Lincoln's Wharf, foot of Battery Street, to foot of Border Street, East Boston.

South Ferry. — From foot of Eastern Avenue to foot of Lewis Street, East Boston.

Chelsea Ferry. — From foot of Hanover Street to Chelsea.

Conveyances out of Boston.

RAILROADS.

The railroads centring at Boston pass through nearly every village of Massachusetts within twenty miles of the city. The several railroads are briefly described below. The time-tables are changed so frequently that it would be useless to insert them in this book. They will at all times be found in the local papers.

Fitchburg Railroad.

From Boston to Fitchburg, fifty miles; double track for the whole distance. Connects at Fitchburg with the Vermont and Massachusetts Railroad to Montreal and the West. When the Hoosac Tunnel is completed, the Fitchburg will constitute the Boston end of that route.

See " Boston Illustrated," a pictorial handbook of Boston.

The principal places on the road and branches are Waltham, Concord, Cambridge, and Fitchburg.

The following shows the stations within twenty miles of Boston, with the distance of each. The station is on Causeway Street.

Station.	Miles.	Station.	Miles.
Ætna Mills,		East Cambridge,	1½
Arlington Street,	6	Fresh Pond,	5
Arsenal,	8	Lincoln,	17
Belmont,	6	Mount Auburn,	5½
Bemis Factory,	9	Prospect Street,	2
Bleachery,	9½	Roberts',	
Brickyard Junction,	4½	Somerville,	2½
Brighton Street,		Stony Brook,	12
Cambridge,	3	Turnpike,	
Charlestown,	1	Union Market,	6½
Chemistry,	10	Waltham,	10
Clematis Brook,		Watertown, ·	8
Concord,	20	Waverley,	7
Concord Turnpike,		Weston,	13

Eastern Railroad.

Main line from station on Causeway Street to Portsmouth, N.H., fifty miles. This road has numerous branches, and it also leases the P. S. and P. Railroad from Portsmouth to Portland. Its cars run through to Bangor, Maine. The principal towns passed through by the Eastern road are Chelsea, Lynn, Salem, Marblehead, Peabody, Newburyport, Gloucester, and Portsmouth.

The following shows the stations within twenty miles of Boston, with the distance to each.

Station.	Miles.	Station.	Miles.
Beverly,	18	Everett,	3
Chelsea,	5	Franklin Park,	7
Cliftondale,	8	Linden,	7½
Danversport,	20	Lynn,	11
East Malden,	6	Lynn Common,	11
East Saugus,	10	Malden,	4

Engravings and Descriptions in " Boston Illustrated."

Station.	Miles.	Station.	Miles.
Maplewood,	5	Saugus,	9
Marblehead,	20	Somerville,	2
Peabody,	18	Swampscott,	13
Revere,	7	West Lynn,	10
Salem,	16		

Boston, Lowell, and Nashua Railroad.

This is the Boston end of the Great Northern route, which has a double track as far as Concord, N.H. It connects with lines to the White Mountains, Northern Vermont, Montreal, and the West. The principal places on the line are Lowell, and Nashua, N.H.

The following alphabetical list shows the stations on the road within twenty miles of Boston, with the distance to each. The station in Boston is on Causeway Street.

Station.	Miles.	Station.	Miles.
Arlington.		Stoneham,	12
College Hill,	4	South Wilmington,	13
East Lexington,		Tewksbury,	19
East Woburn,	9½	Wilmington.	15
Lexington,		Willow Bridge,	3
Medford,	5½	Winchester.	8
Medford Steps,	4½	Winter Hill.	2
Milk Row,	1½	Woburn Centre,	10
Mystic,	7¾	Woburn W. S.,	10
North Woburn,	11½		

Boston and Maine Railroad.

Main line from Boston, station in Haymarket Square, to South-Berwick Junction, seventy-four miles; is extending to Portland, Me., to which point it already connects by the P. S. and P. Railroad, and thence to all parts of Maine and Canada. Also connects to Manchester, Rochester, and the White Mountains. The principal places on its main line are Andover, Lawrence, Haverhill,

See "*Boston Illustrated*," *a pictorial handbook of Boston.*

and Dover, N.H. The following are all the stations on the main line and branches within twenty miles of Boston, alphabetically arranged, with the distance to each : —

Station.	Miles.	Station.	Miles.
Danvers Centre,	18	Reading,	12
Greenwood,	9	Somerville,	2
Lynnfield,	13	Stoneham,	8
Malden,	5	Wakefield,	10
Medford,	5	Wellington's,	3
Melrose.	7	West Danvers,	16
North Danvers,	19	Wilmington,	16
Park Street.	4	Wilmington Junc.,	18
Putnamville,	20	Wyoming,	6

Boston and Providence Railroad.

From Boston to Providence, **forty-four** miles, double track, with several branches. This road connects at Mansfield for New Bedford. It also connects at Providence with the Shore Line to New-York City and all points West and South. The principal places along the line and branches are Dedham, Pawtucket, Taunton, New Bedford, Attleboro', and Providence, R.I. The station in Boston is in Park Square, at the foot of the Common. The following are all the stations on this road and its branches within twenty miles of Boston, with the distance to each : —

Station.	Miles.	Station.	Miles.
Bird's.	17	Monterey.	6
Boylston,	3	Mount Hope,	5
Boylston Street,	3	Readville,	8½
Canton.	14	Roxbury,	2
Central,	6	Sharon,	17½
Dedham,	9½	South Canton.	15
Forest Hills,	4	South Street,	5½
Green Lodge,	11	Spring Dale,	16
Highland,	7	Stoughton,	18
Hyde Park,	7	West Roxbury,	7
Jamaica Plain.	3½		

Engravings and Descriptions in "Boston Illustrated."

Boston, Hartford, and Erie Railroad.

This is a somewhat famous unfinished road. Its main division extends from the station at the foot of Summer Street, Boston, to Putnam, Conn. Its Woonsocket Division enters Boston over the Albany Road, and passengers by that part of the line start from the station at the corner of Beach and Albany Streets. In the appended list of stations within twenty miles of Boston, those on the Woonsocket Division are marked with an asterisk(*).

Station.	Mi'es.	Station.	Miles.
Bird St. (Dorchester),	3	* Medfield,	19½
Blue Hill,	9	Mount Bowdoin,	4
* Brookline,	4	* Needham,	12
* Chapel Station,	3	* Newton Centre,	8
* Charles River,	14½	* Newton Highlands,	9
* Chestnut Hill,	6½	* " Upper Falls,	10
Dorchester,	5	* Reservoir,	5½
* Dover,	16	South Boston,	1
Ellis's,	13	Stoughton Street,	3
Everett's,	15	Tilton's,	18
* Highlandville,	11	Winslow's,	16
Hyde Park,	8	Walpole,	19
* Longwood,	3	West Walpole,	20
Mattapan,	6		

Boston and Albany Railroad.

From Boston to Albany, N.Y., two hundred and two miles, double track all the way, connecting at Albany with the New-York Central for all points West and South. Principal stations on the Boston and Albany Road, Worcester, Palmer, Springfield, and Pittsfield. Branches to Milford, North Adams, and Hudson, N.Y.; connects at Springfield with New Haven, Hartford, and Springfield Road for New York, and with Conn. River R. R. for points northward. The station in Boston is at the corner of Beach and Albany Streets. The following is an alphabetical list of all stations within twenty miles

See "Boston Illustrated," a pictorial handbook of Boston.

of Boston on the Albany Road, with the distance in miles from Boston : —

Station.	Miles.	Station.	Miles.
Allston,	4	Longwood,	3
Auburndale,	10	Natick,	18
Brighton,	5	Newton,	7
Brookline,	4	" Lower Falls,	12
Chapel Station,	3	Newtonville,	8
Cottage Farm,	4	Rice's Crossing,	12
Faneuil.	6	Riverside,	11
Grantville,	13	Wellesley,	15
Lake Crossing,	12	West Newton,	9

Old-Colony Railroad.

Main line from Boston to Newport, sixty-seven miles. Connects at Taunton with New Bedford and Taunton Railroad for New Bedford. This road has numerous branches, and is the Boston terminus of all the roads running along the south shore and to Cape Cod. The principal places reached by it are Taunton, New Bedford, Fall River, Newport, and Plymouth. The Boston station is at the corner of Kneeland and South Streets. The following is a list of all stations on the main line and branches, with the distance of each, within twenty miles of Boston : —

Station.	Miles.	Station.	Miles.
Abington,	19	North Abington,	18
Atlantic,	5½	North Bridgewater,	20
Braintree,	10	North Stoughton,	17
Crescent Avenue,	2	Quincy,	8
East Milton,	6½	Quincy Adams,	8½
East Randolph,	15	Randolph,	15
East Stoughton,	17	Savin Hill,	3
Granite Bridge,	6	South Boston,	½
Harrison Square,	4	South Braintree,	11
Huntington Heights,	18	South Weymouth,	15
Mattapan,	8	Stoughton,	19
Milton Lower Mills,	7	West Quincy,	8
Neponset,	5	Wollaston Heights,	6½

Engravings and Descriptions in "Boston Illustrated."

STEAMBOATS.

In the Harbor.

For Hingham and Hull. — Steamer Rose Standish, from Liverpool Wharf, daily, at 4.30, P.M.

Steamer John Romer, from Liverpool Wharf, daily.

For Nahant. — Steamer Ulysses, from India Wharf, daily.

For Lynn. — Steamer Meta, from India Wharf, daily, at 11, A.M., and 5, P.M.

For Gloucester. — Steamer Sunshine, from north side of Central Wharf, daily, at 1, P.M.

Outside.

For Provincetown. — Steamer George Shattuck, from Central Wharf, Wednesdays and Saturdays, at 9.30, A.M.

For New York. — Metropolitan Line. Steamers Nereus, Glaucus, Ashland, and Neptune, from Central Wharf, Mondays, Wednesdays, and Saturdays, at 5, P.M.

For Philadelphia. — Steamers Aries, Saxon, Roman, and Norman, from Long Wharf, every Wednesday and Saturday, at 3, P.M.

For Norfolk and Baltimore. — Steamers William Crane, William Lawrence, William Kennedy, George Appold, and McClellan, from Central Wharf, Tuesdays and Fridays, at 2.30, P.M.

For Savannah. — Steamers Seminole and Oriental, from T Wharf, on the 10th, 20th, and 30th of each month.

For Portland. — Steamers John Brooks, Forest City, and Montreal, from India Wharf, daily, at 7, P.M.

For Bath and the Kennebec River. — Steamer Star of

the East, from **Union Wharf, Tuesdays** and Fridays, at **6, P.M.**

For Bangor and the Penobscot River. — Steamers Cambridge and Katahdin, from **Foster's Wharf,** Mondays, Tuesdays, Thursdays, and Fridays, at 5.30, **P.M.**

For Eastport, Calais, and St. John, N.B. — Steamers New England and New Brunswick, from Commercial Wharf, Mondays and Thursdays, at 8, **A.M.**

For Halifax and Prince Edward Island. — **Steamers** Alhambra and Oriental, from T Wharf, Saturdays, at **2,** **P.M.**

For Yarmouth, N.S. — Steamer Emperor, every Friday, at 8, **A.M.**

For Liverpool. — Cunard **Steamers Olympus,** Siberia, **Tarifa, Hecla,** Samaria, Palmyra, and others, from **Cunard Wharf,** East Boston, Tuesdays, as the tide serves. Occasional trips on other days as advertised.

Means of Communication.
THE POST-OFFICE.

The Post-office is at present located in the Merchants' Exchange Building, No. 55 State Street. It is open daily, except Sundays, from 7.30, A.M., to 7.30, P.M., and is open all night to those hiring lock-boxes. The stamp-office is open until midnight. Hours of the money-order office from 10, A.M, to 5, P.M. There are two classes of receiving-boxes, for letters only, put up in various parts of the city; from those painted red, letters are collected hourly, from 8, A.M., until 7, P.M., and also at midnight. These boxes are put up at the corner of Pemberton Square and Tremont Street, on the Horticultural-hall building, corner of Montgomery Place, and in Bowdoin Square, in the city proper; also at other horse-car stations. The black boxes are visited at 9, A M., 12,

M , 3, 6.30, and 9, P.M. All boxes are visited at 6 and 9, P.M., only on Sundays. Carriers deliver letters free in all parts of the city, if addressed to street and number, at 7.45 and 11.30, A.M., 2.30, 4.15, and 5.30, P.M. Mails close at the main office, for principal points North and the Canadas at 5 and 11, A.M., and 4, P.M.; for principal points East, at 5 and 11, A.M., 2 and 7, P.M.; for the South and West, at 8, A.M., 2 and 8, P.M.; for Albany and Western New York at 1, A.M., 2 and 8, P.M.; for the West at 1, A.M., 2 and 8, P.M.; for New-York City and the South at 8, A.M., 2 and 8, P.M. Mails for all points in the immediate vicinity of Boston leave every hour between 7, A.M., and 7, P.M.

TELEGRAPH OFFICES.

Western Union.

Principal Office, 83 State Street.

BRANCH OFFICES.

Post-Office.	Warwick House.
Station A Post-Office, So. End.	Tremont House.
Boston Highlands (P. Office)	United States Hotel.
31 State St. (Traveller Build'g).	Boston & Maine Station.
60 Franklin Street.	Boston & Albany Station.
Shoe & Leather Exchange, cor. Pearl and High Sts.	Boston & Providence Station.
Old State House.	Old Colony Station.
St. James Hotel.	Boston & Fitchburg Station.
American House.	Boston & Lowell Station.
Parker House.	Eastern Station.
Revere House.	Boston, Hartford, & Erie Station.

Franklin Telegraph.

Principal Office, 112 State Street.

BRANCH OFFICES.

37 State Street (basement).	64 Franklin Street.
350 Washington Street.	126 Commercial Street.
200 Congress Street.	

See "Boston Illustrated," a pictorial handbook of Boston.

EXPRESSES.

Nearly all local expresses are concentrated in Court Square and at No. 3 Washington Street. The location of the great general express companies is as follows : —

Adams. — Nos. 28 to 40 Court Street.
American Merchants' Union. — No. 94 Washington St.
Eastern. — No. 51 Devonshire Street.
United States and Canada. — Nos. 39 and 40 Court Sq.
Wells, Fargo, & Co. — No. 96 Washington Street.

Places of Interest.

Public Buildings.

The following public buildings in and about Boston may be visited and examined. Where nothing to the contrary is stated, they may be visited at any hour and on any day, except Sunday.

City Hall. — On School Street.
State House. — Beacon Street. The cupola may be visited any day, except during the session of the Legislature. The rotunda and offices are open at all times during the daytime.
County Court House. — Court Square.
Suffolk-County Jail. — Charles Street, near Cambridge Street.
Faneuil Hall. — Always open. Entrance at east end of the hall.
Faneuil Hall (Quincy) Market. — Between North and South Market Streets. Open during every day.

Engravings and Descriptions in "Boston Illustrated."

Public Library. — Boylston Street, near Tremont. Open to all, from 9, A.M., during every day and evening, except Sundays.

Boston Athenæum. — Beacon Street, near Somerset Street. Open every day from 9, A.M., until 6, P.M. This is a private library, but visitors are admitted.

Boston Athenæum Gallery. — In Athenæum Building, as above. Open during every day, except Sundays, on payment of a small fee.

Old State House. — Head of State Street. This is not now a public building, but it possesses a great deal of historic interest. It may be visited at any time.

City Hospital. — Harrison Avenue, opposite Worcester Square. Admittance only by permit.

Massachusetts General Hospital. — Blossom Street. Admittance only by permit.

Beacon-Hill Reservoir. — In the square bounded by Hancock, Derne, Temple, and Mount-Vernon Streets. A solid granite structure worthy to be examined. Visitors are allowed to ascend to the top of the reservoir, on application to the janitor at the upper end on Hancock Street.

Custom House. — State Street. Admission during business hours.

Post-office. — State Street. Admission during any hour of the day or night.

United States Court House. — Corner of Tremont Street and Temple Place.

Almshouse. — South Boston.

House of Correction. — South Boston.

House of Industry. — South Boston.

House of Refuge. — South Boston.

Insane Hospital. — South Boston.

Perkins Institution for the Blind. — Broadway, South Boston. Admission by permit, to be obtained on application at No. 20 Bromfield Street.

See "Boston Illustrated," a pictorial handbook of Boston.

Boston Society of Natural History. — Corner of Berkeley and Boylston Streets. Admission to all on Wednesdays and Saturdays, between the hours of 10, A.M., and 2, P.M.

Institute of Technology. — Boylston Street, between Berkeley and Clarendon.

Masonic Temple. — Corner of Boylston and Tremont Streets.

New Odd Fellows' Hall. — Corner of Berkeley and Tremont Streets.

Horticultural Hall. — Corner of Tremont and Bromfield Streets.

New Post-office. — Corner of Water and Devonshire Streets.

Charitable Mechanics' Association Building. — Corner of Bedford and Chauncy Streets.

Historic-Genealogical Society. — 17 Somerset Street.

Washington Market. — Corner of Washington and Lenox Streets.

Sub-Treasury. — Over the Post-office, State Street

Statues and Monuments.

Many of the following are mentioned elsewhere in this Guide Book. No monuments to be found in any of the burying-grounds are included in this list.

Soldiers' Monument. — Foundation laid on Flag-staff Hill, on the Common.

Statue of Everett. — Public-Garden, Beacon-street side.

Equestrian Statue of Washington. — Public Garden, Arlington-street entrance.

Venus rising from the Sea. — Public Garden, near Arlington-street entrance.

Ether Monument. — Public Garden, north-west part.

Statue of Franklin. — In front of City Hall.

Statue of Andrew. — Doric Hall, State House.

Statue of Washington. — Doric Hall, State House.

Engravings and Descriptions in " Boston Illustrated."

46 *Strangers' New Guide*

Statue of Mann. — In front of State House.
Statue of Webster. — In front of State House.
Statue of Hamilton. — Commonwealth Avenue, near Arlington Street.
Statue of Aristides. — Louisburg Square.
Statue of Columbus. — Louisburg Square.
Statue of Beethoven. — Music Hall.
Bunker-hill Monument. — Bunker-hill Square, Charlestown.
Chelsea Soldiers' Monument. — Chelsea Common.
Cambridge Soldiers' Monument. — Cambridge Common.

Parks and Squares.

The following are the principal parks and open spaces in Boston, and their location.

The Common. — Bounded by Tremont, Boylston, Charles, Beacon, and Park Streets.
The Public Garden. — Bounded by Boylston, Arlington, Beacon, and Charles Streets.
Commonwealth Avenue. — From Arlington Street westward.
Louisburg Square. — Bounded by Mount-Vernon, West-Cedar, and Pinckney Streets.
Haymarket Square. — At the junction of Union, Charlestown, and Merrimac Streets.
Dock Square. — Head of Washington Street.
Union Park. — From 93 Shawmut Avenue to Tremont Street.
Blackstone Square. — Bounded by West-Brookline, Washington, and West-Newton Streets and Shawmut Avenue.
Franklin Square. — Bounded by East-Brookline, Washington, East-Newton, and James Streets.
Rutland Square. — From 703 Tremont Street to Columbus Avenue.

See "*Boston Illustrated*," *a pictorial handbook of Boston.*

Concord Square. — From 725 Tremont Street to Columbus Avenue.

Worcester Square. — From 1498 Washington Street to 799 Harrison Avenue.

Chester Square. — From 1541 Washington Street to 772 Tremont Street.

Chester Park. — **From** 1655 Washington Street to **773** Albany Street.

West-Chester Park. — From 781 Tremont Street to Columbus Avenue.

Eliot Square. — Junction of Washington, Dudley, and Centre Streets, Roxbury.

Egleston Square. — From 1076 Shawmut Avenue to 387 Walnut Avenue, Roxbury.

Maverick Square. — Bounded by Lewis, Maverick, Meridian, Chelsea, and Sumner Streets, East Boston.

Central Square. — Junction of Border, Liverpool, Meridian, Bennington, and Saratoga Streets, East Boston.

Independence Square. — Bounded by M, Second, and N Streets, and Broadway, South Boston.

The Principal Wharves.

Boston is surrounded with wharves, from Warren Bridge, on Charles River, to Federal-street Bridge, across Fort-Point Channel. There are also important wharves in South Boston, and some of the most extensive in the harbor at East Boston. Upon most of these are long lines of substantial warehouses. In this place we can but mention a few of the more important wharves, as follows, beginning at the northern part of the city and proceeding southward : —

Constitution. — From 411 Commercial Street.

Lincoln's. — From 365 Commercial Street.

Union. — From 323 Commercial Street.

Sargent's. — From 293 Commercial Street, foot of Fleet Street.

Lewis. — From 221 Commercial Street.
Commercial. — From 171 Commercial Street.
T. — From 46 Long Wharf.
Long. — Foot of State Street.
Central. — From India, foot of Milk Street.
India. — From foot of India Street.
Rowe's. — From 144 Broad Street.
Liverpool. — From 280 Broad Street.
Russia. — From 306 Broad Street.
Boston. — From First Street, South Boston.
Ferry. — Foot of Lewis Street, East Boston.
Eastern-Railroad. — From Marginal, opposite Orleans Street, East Boston.
Cunard. — From Marginal, opposite Orleans Street, East Boston.
Grand-Junction Wharves. — From Marginal Street, East Boston.

Markets.

Faneuil Hall. — Faneuil-hall building and Quincy building, between North and South Market Streets.
Blackstone. — From 72 to 92 Blackstone Street.
Lakeman. — Corner of Blackstone and North Streets.
Union. — Union Street, between North and Hanover Streets.
Central. — No. 50 North Street.
Merrimac. — Corner of Merrimac and Market Streets.
Suffolk. — Corner of Portland and Sudbury Streets.
Boylston. — Corner of Washington and Boylston Sts.
St. Charles. — Corner of Beach and Lincoln Streets.
Williams. — Corner of Washington and East-Dover Streets.
Washington. — Corner of Washington and Lenox Sts.
Tremont. — No. 923 Tremont Street.
Washington. — No. 390 Broadway, South Boston.

See " *Boston Illustrated,*" *a pictorial handbook of Boston.*

Libraries.

American Academy of **Arts and Sciences**, Athenæum Building, Beacon Street.
American Congregational Association, No. 40 Winter Street.
Boston Athenæum, Athenæum Building, Beacon Street.
Boston Library Society, No. 13 Boylston Place.
Boston Public Library, Boylston St., near Tremont. Open to all.
Boston Society of Natural History, Berkeley Street, between Newbury and Boylston.
Boston Young Men's Christian Association, No. 5 Tremont Temple, Tremont Street, near School.
Boston Young Men's Christian Union, No. 309 Washington Street.
Dorchester Athenæum, corner Pleasant and Cottage Streets (D.).
Franklin Typographical Society, No. 46 Washington Street.
General Theological Library, No. 12 West Street.
Harvard Musical Association, No. 12 Pemberton Square.
Law Library, No. 14 Court House, Court Square.
Massachusetts Historical Society, Tremont Street, between Pemberton Square and Beacon Street.
Massachusetts Horticultural Society, cor. Trem't and Bromfield Sts.
Mattapan Library, corner Park and Exchange Streets (D.).
Mechanic Apprentices' Library Association, No. 43 Chauncy Street.
Medical Library, No. 36 Temple Place.
Mercantile Library Association, No. 1179 Washington Street.
New Church Free Library, No. 2 Hamilton Place.
New-England Historical Genealogical Society, Somerset Street, near Allston.
Roxbury Athenæum, No. 27 Guild Row (R.).
Social Law Library, No. 14 Court House, Court Square.

Daily Newspapers.

Boston **Daily** Advertiser (morning), No. 29 Court Street.
Boston Post (morning), corner of Water and Devonshire Streets.
Boston Daily Globe (morning), No. 92 Washington Street.
Boston Daily Journal (morning and evening), No. 120 Wash. **Street.**
Boston Herald (morning and evening), No. 103 Washington Street.
Boston Daily Times (morning and evening), No. 12 School Street.
Boston Daily News (morning and evening), No. 4 Province Court.
Boston Transcript (evening), No. 150 Washington Street.
Boston Traveller (evening), No. 31 State Street.

Prominent Churches.

First Church (Cong. Un.), Marlboro', corner Berkeley, Rufus Ellis.
King's Chapel (Cong. Un.), Tremont, cor. School, Henry W. Foote.
South Congregational (Cong. Un.), Union-Park St., Edward E. Hale.
Church of the Disciples (Cong. Un.), W. Brookline St., J. F. Clarke.
West-Boston Society (Cong. Un.), Lynde Street, Cyrus A. Bartol.

Engravings and Descriptions in "Boston Illustrated."

4

Old South Church, (Cong. Trin.) Wash., c. Milk, G. W. Blagden and Jacob M. Manning.
Park-street Ch. (Cong. Trin.), Tremont, c. Park, Wm. H. H. Murray.
Central Church (Cong. Trin.), Berkeley, c. Newbury, J. De Witt.
Shawmut Church (Cong. Trin.), Tremont, c. Brookline, E. B. Webb.
Christ Church (Epis.), Salem Street, Henry Burroughs, jun.
Trinity Church (Epis.), Summer, corner Hawley, Phillips Brooks.
Church of the Advent (Epis.), Bowdoin Street.
Emanuel Church (Epis.), Newbury Street, A. H. Vinton.
Grace Methodist-Episcopal Church, Temple St., A. Canoll.
Tremont-street Methodist-Episcopal, Tremont St., D. Steele.
First Baptist Church, Somerset St., R. H. Neale & J. T. Beckley.
Clarendon-st. Ch. (Bapt.), Clarendon, c. Montgom'y, A. J. Gordon.
Union-Temple Church (Bapt.), Tremont Temple, J. D. Fulton.
Shawmut-avenue Church (Bapt.), Shawmut Avenue, G. C. Lorimer.
Second Presbyterian, Beach, cor. Harrison Ave., J. B. Dunn.
Second Universalist, School St., A. A. Miner, and H. I. Cushman.
East Boston Universalist, Central Square, Geo. H. Vibbert.
New-Jerusalem Church (Sweden'n), Bowdoin Street, James Reed.
Cathedral Chapel of Holy Cross (Rom. Cath.), Castle Street.
Church of the Holy Trinity (Rom. Cath.), Suffolk Street.
Church of the Immaculate Conception (Rom. Cath.), Harrison Ave.

Places of Amusement.

Theatres.

Boston Theatre. — The largest theatre in Boston. It is conducted on the "star" system. There is a very good stock company, and the theatre always has some fresh attractions, — a great star actor, a spectacular drama, or German, Italian, or English opera. It is situated on Washington Street, near West. J. B. Booth, manager.

Globe Theatre. — One of the most beautiful and completely-furnished theatres in the country. It is conducted partly on the stock company and partly on the star principle. The orchestra at this theatre is very fine, and the acting is almost uniformly good. It is on Washington

Street, near Essex. Arthur Cheney, proprietor ; W. R. Floyd, manager.

Boston Museum. — This is the favorite orthodox theatre of Boston, and is situated on Tremont Street, near Court. It is the home of comedy in Boston, and discards the star system altogether. It is with this theatre that the famous comedian, William Warren, has been connected so long. The company is excellent. R. M. Field, manager.

Howard Athenæum. — Situated on Howard Street. This was once a theatre for the legitimate drama. It is now wholly given up to variety entertainments, and is nightly crowded with the lovers of that class of amusement. The attractions, which are of every variety, from performing dogs up to the latest sensation in negro minstrelsy, succeed each other with bewildering rapidity.

St. James Theatre. — This theatre has gone by various names. It has lately passed under a new management, and has been used for a series of the lighter class of entertainments, — burlesques, French opera, and the like. It is on Washington Street, near Bennet.

Music and Lecture Halls.

The following are some of the more important of the halls used for public concerts, lectures, and similar entertainments.

Music Hall. — No. 15 Winter Street. This is the largest hall in Boston. It is constantly in use for concerts, lectures, fairs, and other entertainments. Admission can be obtained at any time during the day, on the payment of a fee. The hall is well worthy of a visit by all who have not entered it.

Bumstead Hall. — This is a small hall beneath the

grand Music Hall, and is often used in connection with the latter. It is also the head-quarters of the Handel and Haydn Society, and the place for its rehearsals.

Horticultural Hall. — There are two fine halls in the Horticultural Building, corner of Tremont and Bromfield Streets. They are used for chamber concerts, fairs, parties, dances, lectures, and religious discourses on certain Sunday afternoons.

Faneuil Hall. — In Faneuil-hall Square. This historic hall is open to visitors throughout the day. It is used only for public meetings ; and the use of it is granted by the city government, if at all, without fee.·

Wesleyan-Association Hall. — Bromfield Street, opposite Province. This is a small but very pleasant hall, often used for concerts, for lectures, and for meetings of associations.

Brackett's Hall. — The location of this hall is excellent. It is at No. 409 Washington, near Boylston Street. Its shape is hardly the best for a public hall, but it has nevertheless been much used of late for concerts and other entertainments for audiences of a few hundred.

Tremont Temple. — Tremont Street, near School. This is a very large and fine hall, used for religious exercises on Sunday, and very frequently during the week for conventions, lectures, readings, and concerts. It was in this hall that Charles Dickens gave his readings on his last visit to America.

Meionaon. — A small hall under Tremont Temple.

Institute Hall. — No. 113 Dudley Street, Roxbury. The largest and finest hall at the Highlands, and used for all purposes to which a public hall is devoted.

John A. Andrew Hall. — Corner of Chauncy and Essex Streets. A small hall used for various purposes.

Lowell Institute. — Rear of 223 Washington Street. This hall is the place where most of the Lowell-Institute free lectures are delivered.

See "Boston Illustrated," a pictorial handbook of Boston.

The City Government for 1872.

Mayor. — WILLIAM GASTON.
Chairman Board of Aldermen. — Samuel Little.
President Common Council. — M. F. Dickinson, Jr.
City Clerk. — S. F. McCleary.
Clerk of Committees. — James M. Bugbee.
City Solicitor. — John P. Healy.
City Treasurer. — Frederick U. Tracy.
Auditor. — Alfred T. Turner.
City Physician. — Samuel A. Green, M. D.
Port Physician. — S. H. Durgin.
Superintendent of Streets. — Charles Harris.
Superintendent of Health. — G. W. Forrist.ll.
President Water Board. — Charles II. Allen.
Chairman Overseers of Poor. — Frederick W. Lincoln.
President Board of Directors for Public Institutions. —
    J. Putnam Bradlee.
Street Commissioners. — Joseph Smith, Isaac S. Burrell,
    Christopher A. Connor.

POLICE DEPARTMENT,

Chief of Police. — Edward H. Savage.
Deputy Chief. — James Quinn.

Police Stations.

1. No. 209 Hanover, near Cross Street.
2. No. 21 Court Square, corner Williams Court.
3. Joy Street, near Cambridge.
4. No. 23 La Grange Street.
5. East-Dedham Street.
6. Broadway, near C Street (South Boston).
7. Paris Street (East Boston).
8. Corner Commercial and Salutation Streets.
9. Old City Hall (Roxbury).
10. Junction Washington and Tremont Streets.
11. Hancock Street (Dorchester).

Engravings and Descriptions in "Boston Illustrated."

FIRE DEPARTMENT.

The Fire Department, head-quarters in City Hall, is under the direction of John S. Damrell, Chief Engineer, and fourteen assistant engineers, all of whom are elected annually by the City Council. There are twenty-one steam fire-engines, each officered by an engineer, a driver, a foreman, and seven hosemen, — the first three permanently employed, the others called out by an alarm. Six engines are located in Boston proper, three in East Boston, three in South Boston, three in Roxbury, and six in Dorchester. The Hose Companies are ten in number, each officered by a driver, a foreman, and seven hosemen, the driver only being permanently employed : six hose carriages are located in Boston proper, one in East Boston, two in South Boston, and one in Roxbury. The Hook and Ladder Companies are seven in number, — two in Boston proper, one in East Boston, two in South Boston, and two in Dorchester : the companies consist of a driver, a foreman, an assistant foreman, and axemen, rakemen, and members. There are also two " Extinguisher " Corps, both in Boston proper, and an Insurance Brigade. The whole force of the department numbers 472 men.

Fire Alarms.

The fire-alarm department is under the charge of J. F. Kennard, Superintendent, at the City Hall ; and alarms are given by telegraph from the dome of the City Hall by striking, upon the alarm-bells and upon the gongs in the engine-houses, the number of the box from which the alarm has been telegraphed to the central station. The system is explained as follows : to announce the existence of a fire near Box No. 41 (Old South Church), the bells will strike *four,* make a pause of a few seconds, then strike *one,* thus : 4 — 1. This will be repeated at intervals of

---

See "Boston Illustrated," a pictorial handbook of Boston."

about one minute. For a fire near Box **No. 145** (South-Boston Point), the bells will strike *one*, make a pause, then strike *four*, another pause, then strike *five*, thus : 1—4—5.

Second alarms are sounded by striking ten blows. Third **alarms** are sounded by striking twelve blows twice, thus : 12 — 12.

In cases where the entire department is required, alarms are sounded by striking twelve blows three times, thus : 12 —12 —12.

In cases where hook-and-ladder companies *only* are wanted, signal to be given by striking ten blows once, with the number of the company struck twice, thus : Hook and Ladder No. 1, 10 —1—1. Hook and Ladder No. 4, 10 —4— 4. Hook and Ladder No. 7, 10— 7—7.

If more than one hook-and-ladder company is wanted, the signal will be given thus : Hook and Ladder 1 and 3, 10 —1—1—3 — 3. Hook and Ladder 2 and 4, 10 — 2 — 2 —4 — 4. Hook and Ladder 5 and 7, 10 — 5 — 5 — 7 — 7. The following shows the location of all the alarm-boxes in the city : —

IN THE CITY PROPER.

NO.	LOCALITY OF BOXES.
2.	Corner Charter Street and Phipps Place.
3.	Corner Hull and Snowhill Streets.
4.	Causeway Street (B. & M. Freight Depot).
5.	Corner Causeway and Lowell Streets.
6.	Corner Leverett and Willard Streets.
7.	Corner Poplar and Spring Streets.
8.	Merrimac House.
9.	Constitution Wharf.
12.	Corner Cooper and Endicott Streets.
13.	Corner Hanover and Richmond Streets.
14.	Corner Commercial Street and Eastern Avenue.
15.	Corner Commercial and Richmond Streets.
16.	East End of Faneuil Hall.
17.	Corner Hanover and Salem Streets.
18.	Quincy House.
19.	Haymarket Square (B. & M. Depot).
21.	Corner Sudbury and Hawkins Streets.
23.	Corner Cambridge and Bowdoin Streets.
24.	North-Russell Street (Church).

NO.   LOCALITY OF BOXES.

25. West City Stables.
26. Corner Cambridge and West-Cedar Streets.
27. River Street (Steamer House No. 10).
28. Corner Beacon and Spruce Streets.
29. Corner Beacon and Clarendon Streets.
31. Corner Beacon and Beaver Streets.
32. Corner Pinckney and Anderson Streets.
34. Corner Hancock and Myrtle Streets.
35. Beacon Street, opposite Somerset.
36. Court Square (Police Station No. 2).
37. Corner India Street and Central Wharf.
41. Corner Washington and Milk Streets.
42. Corner Winter Street and Central Place.
43. Corner Washington and Bedford Streets.
45. Corner Federal and Channing Streets.
46. Corner Milk and Oliver Streets.
47. Corner Broad Street and Rowe's Wharf.
48. Boston H. & E. R. R. Station.
51. Corner Purchase and Pearl Streets.
52. Corner Bedford and Lincoln Streets.
53. Corner Washington and Boylston Streets.
54. Corner Beach and Hudson Streets.
56. Corner Kneeland and South Streets (O. C. Depot).
57. Hudson Street (Hose House No. 2).
58. Harvard Street (B. & A. Freight Depot).
59. East Street (School House).
61. Warrenton Street, near Tremont.
62. Pleasant Street (Providence Depot).
63. Berkeley Street, near Commonwealth Avenue.
64. Washington Street and Indiana Place.
65. Corner Harrison Avenue and Seneca Streets.
67. Corner Washington and Common Streets.
68. Corner Harrison Avenue and Wareham Street.
69. Corner Beacon and Exeter Streets.
71. Corner Warren Avenue and Berkeley Street.
72. Washington Street (Steamer House No. 3).
73. Corner Shawmut Avenue and Waltham Street.
74. Dedham Street (Police Station No. 5).
75. Shawmut Avenue (Hose House No. 5).
76. Corner Tremont and Rutland Streets.
78. Parker Street and Railroad Crossing.
79. Corner of Dover and Albany Streets.
81. West-Canton and Appleton Streets.
82. Northampton Street (Hose House No. 4).
83. Corner Tremont and Camden Streets.
84. South City Stables.
85. Tremont and Paul Streets.

The numbers from 121 to 145, inclusive, are those of boxes in South Boston; from 151 to 178, of boxes in East Boston; from 212 to 257, in Roxbury; and from 312 to 341, in Dorchester.

See "Boston Illustrated," a pictorial handbook of Boston.

PUBLIC BATHING PLACES,

The public baths are open June 1st, and are kept open daily until September 30th each year, and are free to all. Those marked with an asterisk (*) are for women and girls. All the others are for men and boys.

1. West-Boston Bridge, foot of Cambridge.
2. Craigie's Bridge, foot of Leverett.
3. Charles-river Bridge, near Causeway.
*4. Warren Bridge.
5. East Boston, Sectional Dock, Border Street.
*6. East Boston, Sectional Dock, 96 Border Street.
7. Federal-street Bridge.
8. Mount-Washington-avenue Bridge.
*9. South Boston, foot of 5th Street.
10. South Boston, south end L Street.
11. Dover-street Bridge, South Pier.
*12. Dover-street Bridge, South Pier.
13. Cabot Street, Roxbury.
*14. Cabot Street, Roxbury.
15. Swett Street, South Bay.
16. Commercial Point, Dorchester.
17. Maverick Street, East Boston.

Hotels and Restaurants.

Hotels.

The following partial list of the hotels in Boston may be of use to strangers stopping in the city. The houses are classified. Those which are wholly or chiefly boarding or family hotels are marked with an asterisk (*). Those which are large and first-class in every respect are printed in SMALL CAPITALS, and those which are smaller in size, though perhaps equally worthy of patronage, are printed in *italics*.

Adams,	No. 371 Washington Street.
* Albion,	Cor. Beacon and Tremont Streets.
AMERICAN,	No. 56 Hanover Street.
Anderson,	Cor. Essex St. and Harrison Ave.
Avon,	No. 19 Avon Street.
Boston,	Cor. Beach St. and Harrison Ave.
Campbell,	No. 6 Wilson's Lane.
Central,	No. 4 Central Square (E. B.).
City,	No. 55 Brattle Street.
* Clarendon,	No. 523 Tremont Street.
* Commonwealth,	No. 1511 Washington Street.
* Coolidge,	Bowdoin Square.
Creighton,	No. 245 Tremont Street.
Essex,	No. 16 Essex Street.
* Evans,	No. 175 Tremont Street.
* Everett,	Cor. Washington and Camden Sts.
* Hotel Bellevue,	No. 17 Beacon Street.
International,	No. 415 Washington Street.
* La Grange,	No. 6 La Grange Street.
* Lancaster,	Corner Wash. and E. Concord Sts.
Marlboro',	No. 227 Washington Street.
Maverick,	No. 24 Maverick Square (E. B.).
Merrimac,	Cor. Merrimac and Friend Streets.
National,	Cor. Blackstone and Cross Streets.
New-England,	Cor. Clinton and Blackstone Sts.
* NORFOLK,	Eliot Square (R.).
Park,	No. 7 Central Court.
PARKER,	No. 60 School Street.
Parks,	No. 187 Washington Street.
Province,	No. 1 Province Court.
Quincy,	No. 1 Brattle Square.
REVERE,	Bowdoin Square.
Sears,	Court Avenue.

See "Boston Illustrated," a pictorial handbook of Boston.

Selwyn,	No. 29 Harrison Avenue.
Sherman,	Court Square.
* St. Denis,	No. 1421 Washington Street.
St. Elmo,	No. 27 Boylston Street.
St. James,	Franklin Square.
Temple,	Nos. 8 and 9 Bowdoin Square.
Trainer's,	Cor. Wash. and West-Dover Streets.
Tremont,	Cor. Tremont and Beacon Streets.
United States,	Cor. Beach and Lincoln Streets.
Warwick,	No. 1028 Washington Street.
* Winthrop,	Cor. Bowdoin and Allston Streets.
Young's,	Court Avenue.

Restaurants and Cafes.

The stranger in Boston who cannot find a place to satisfy his hunger in any part of the city must be extremely unfortunate. For the guidance of those who do not know where to go with an assurance that they will be well served, we insert a list of cafés, restaurants, and confectioners of the best reputation in various parts of Boston; but as the list is short, and does not pretend to be complete, the absence of any saloon or eating-house from it is not to be taken as in any way prejudicial to it. Those where ladies are wont to resort are marked with an asterisk (*).

Parker House, gentlemen's dining-room, *ladies' dining-room, and café in the basement, School Street.

**Tremont-House Café*, corner of Tremont and Beacon Streets.

**Revere-House Café*, Bowdoin Square.

Copeland's, No. 4 Tremont Row.

Copeland's, No. 208 Washington Street.

Copeland's, Tremont Street, opposite Park Street.

Young's Hotel, Court Avenue.

**Weber's*, No. 25 Temple Place.

**Fera's*, No. 343 Washington Street.
Kendall's, No. 8 Congress Square.
Stumcke & Goodwin, No. 9 Brattle Street.
**Mrs. Harrington's*, No. 13 School Street.
*La Grange, corner of La Grange and Tremont Streets.
**Dooling's*, Nos. 1247 and 1249 Washington Street.
**Young Women's Christian Association* (ladies only),
No. 25 Beach Street.

THE PEACE JUBILEE.

The International Peace Jubilee, beginning in Boston on the 17th of June, 1872, is the legitimate outgrowth of the magnificent success of the first Jubilee in 1869. Mr. Gilmore projected that grand festival in 1867, and was two years in preparing for it. Immediately after its close he began to lay his plans for a repetition of the feat on a grander scale. The result we may see to-day in the enormous building, covering four and a half acres of ground, at the crossing of the Albany and the Providence Railroads. It would require more space than could be devoted to the subject to give any thing approaching a full description of the building and the plan of operations for the three weeks beginning with the 17th of June and ending on the 6th of July. We can merely refer to some of the interesting points in connection with the Jubilee.

Officers of the Jubilee.

Executive Committee. — ALEXANDER H. RICE, *President;* EBEN D. JORDAN, *Treasurer;* HENRY G. PARKER, *Secretary;* LEWIS RICE, HENRY MASON, JOSEPH H. CHADWICK, M. M. BALLOU, EDWARD SANDS, JOSEPH F. PAUL, SAMUEL LITTLE, GEORGE H. DAVIS, CHARLES W. SLACK, G. WETHERBEE, OLIVER DITSON, M. F. DICKINSON, JR.

See "Boston Illustrated," a pictorial handbook of Boston.

Finance Committee. — SAMUEL LITTLE, *Chairman.*
Building Committee. — GEORGE H. DAVIS, *Chairman.*
Committee on Decorations. — M. P. KENNARD, *Chairman.*
Committee on Printing. — HENRY G. PARKER, *Chairman.*
Committee on *Music.* — JOHN C. HAYNES, *Chairman.*
Committee on *Transportation.* — A. A. FOLSOM, *Chair-*
-*man.*
Committee on Reception of the *Press.* — **J. R.** OSGOOD,
Chairman.
City Committee. — THOS. L. JENKS, *Chairman.*
Projector. — P. S. GILMORE.
Superintendent of Chorus. — EBEN TOURJÉE.
Superintendent of Orchestra. — J. THOMAS BALDWIN.
Superintendent of the Coliseum. — JOSEPH H. CHADWICK.
Conductors. — P. S. GILMORE, CARL ZERRAHN, FRANZ
ABT, JOHANN STRAUSS.

The Coliseum.

The building in which the Jubilee is held is called the
Coliseum, and is built on the same general plan as the
Coliseum of 1869. The architect is William G. Preston.
It was at first intended to erect a more magnificent structure; but the wind played havoc with the part already
erected on the new plan, and the time was so short, that
it was necessary to resort to the old model. The Coliseum
has an extreme length of 550 feet, and a width of 350 feet.
It contains a parquet, surrounded by galleries on every
side, — that at one end being given up to the chorus and
orchestra. Surrounding the building there are immense
retiring, ante, reception, and other rooms. The height of
the building to the crown of the roof is about 115 feet.
The capacity of the building for audience, musicians, and
chorus has not been accurately calculated; but the figures
showing the size of the building indicate that its capacity
must be very great.

Engravings and Descriptions in "Boston Illustrated."

The seats for the chorus occupy the easterly end of the building for a distance of 240 feet forward from the end wall, arranged in the manner of an amphitheatre (rising some 26 feet) around the place allotted to the orchestra. Radial aisles of ample width give access to the various portions of the chorus territory, connecting with other semi-circular aisles of greater width, into which the stairways open. Very ample stairway accommodation has been provided for the chorus; no less than nine, having an aggregate width of 108 feet, offering their broad passages for the speedy and comfortable entrance and exit of the singers and musicians, the latter being placed in front of the chorus.

The parquet is 235 feet long by 200 feet in width, and is divided into sections discriminated on the plan by letters. It has a smooth double floor of spruce; and the seating is to be made in such a manner as to be easily removed upon the occasion of the grand ball. The parquet is surrounded upon three sides by promenades 25 feet in width under the side and end galleries. These galleries are 75 feet deep, being 10 feet from the parquet floor in front, and rising backward to the walls at a gradual elevation of two and a half inches in every foot. In each of these galleries there will be rows of seats longitudinally, then an aisle, and then other similar rows of seats. Back of the rear row is a promenade-gallery 12 feet wide, and extending all the way round the building, 1,800 feet. These galleries are accessible by means of 12 broad stairways leading from the outside doors; so that those holding gallery tickets reach their seats without being in the way of those who are to sit in the parquet.

Entrance to the building is effected by 12 doorways, each 25 feet in width, and six others of somewhat smaller dimensions. Passages of corresponding width extend directly into the parquet promenade, and corridors

See "*Boston Illustrated*," *a pictorial handbook of Boston.*

of similar width give access to the chorus waiting-rooms. The Coliseum has been very finely decorated by C. W. Roeth and L. Hollis.

The Organ.

The organ, ouilt for this Coliseum by J. H. Wilcox & Co., is the most powerful instrument ever constructed. It fills a space 30 feet wide and 20 feet deep; and one of the pipes reaches to a height of 43 feet from the gallery base. The organ has no case; and all the pipes are visible, except those in the swell organ. A gas engine supplies the power for blowing the organ, and the eight pumps which throw air into the wind-chest have a capacity of 1,280 cubic feet a minute. The organ has two banks of keys and one of pedals. The great organ has fifteen stops, the swell organ seven, and the pedal seven. Two of the stops in the pedal organ are novel, one being an invention of the builder, and the other — the megalophonia, or great sound — being the only one of the kind in the country, and having 32 foot-pipes. There are also 15 mechanical registers.

The Orchestra.

The orchestra is the largest ever gathereu. All the musicians, including the bands, form the grand orchestra. From this is formed a smaller select orchestra. The grand orchestra consists of 2,000 musicians; and these musicians come, not only from Massachusetts, New York, Pennsylvania, Ohio, Illinois, and the far West and South, but from Canada, from England, from Ireland, from France and Germany. The select orchestra, consisting of Strauss and his orchestra of 50, and over 800 others from this country, will be called upon to play the symphonies, and other selections of the less popular class of music. It is

---

Engravings and Descriptions in "Boston Illustrated."

made up as follows, the famous orchestra of Strauss not being included in the list of instruments: First violins, 200 ; second violins, 150 ; violas, 100 ; violoncellos, 100 ; contra bassi, 100; flutes, 24 ; clarinets, 24 ; oboes, 20 ; fagotti, 20 ; trumpets, 24 ; French horns, 24 ; trombones, 24 ; tubas, 4 ; tympani, 6 ; side drums, 4 ; bass drums, 2 ; big drum, 1 ; triangles, 2.

The Soloists and Select Chorus.

The list of soloists has not been completed at the time of going to press. Among those already engaged are Madame Rudersdorff and Madame Peschka-Leutner. The famous pianist, Madame Arabella Goddard, has also been engaged. A choice selection of the best solo-singers in the country has been made ; and these are to be massed for the performance of solo parts. The arrangements for this part of the entertainment are not complete.

The Chorus.

The eagerness of musical people to engage in the Jubilee was most strikingly illustrated in the history of the chorus. In three weeks from the opening of the list for a chorus of 20,000, the entire number was procured, and many more were applying vainly for admission. Massachusetts, of course, furnishes the largest contingent. All the New-England States are represented, however, together with New York, Pennsylvania, New Jersey, Maryland, Illinois, Iowa, Wisconsin, Missouri, California, and New Brunswick. The whole number of societies is 165, and the aggregate number of voices is fully 20,000.

BOSTON ILLUSTRATED:

A Pictorial Handbook of Boston and its Surroundings.

———————◆———————

Boston and its suburbs, though noted for picturesque beauty and scenes rich in memorable associations, have never been adequately described and illustrated. Thousands of the residents of Boston, though proud of the city for its numerous attractive features, and proverbially jealous of its good reputation, are unacquainted with the precise locality, historical interest, and distinctive characteristics of many buildings and objects more or less famous in the annals of Boston. For these, for the strangers who in greater or smaller numbers throng Boston constantly, and especially for the convenience of the multitudes drawn to Boston to attend the World's Peace Jubilee, to whom the sights of the city and its vicinity are of hardly less interest than the vast proportions of the Coliseum and the colossal musical performances of the occasion, Messrs. JAMES R. OSGOOD & Co. have prepared a compact, yet full, handbook, entitled, "Boston Illustrated." It is vastly fuller and more attractive than any guide-book of Boston heretofore published, and describes those scenes, objects, and buildings by which the city is most adorned or distinguished, and whatever is likely to engage the attention of visitors. This book is a full, reliable, interesting, and handsome work, indispensable both to strangers and residents, and worthy of the good fame of the city.

———————

Price, Fifty Cents.

———————

BOSTON IL

A Pictorial Handbook of

"BOSTON ILLUSTRATED" contains nearly one hundred and fifty Illustrations of those Buildings, Monuments, and Scenes which most persons, visitors or residents, would desire to see pictorially represented. These Illustrations have been expressly prepared for "BOSTON ILLUSTRATED" with great care to secure accuracy as well as picturesqueness. They include Faneuil Hall, — the "Cradle of Liberty," — the Old State House, from whose balcony Samuel Adams announced the Declaration of Independence, the Old South Church, the Old Corner Bookstore, Bunker-Hill Monument, and other memorials of the Revolutionary era; Copp's Hill, King's Chapel, and the Old Granary Burying-ground; the noteworthy public buildings, such as the State House, City Hall, Masonic Temple, Public Library, Athenæum; other structures of beauty, or possessing some characteristics or associations which render them objects of special interest, — churches, halls, hotels, theatres; the Chestnut-Hill Reservoir in Brookline, the Stand-Pipe in Roxbury, and other adjuncts of the City Water-Works; Harvard University buildings at Cambridge, and the residences of some famous men of letters in and about Boston; views of some of the substantial business-blocks of the city. These, and a host of other views, are pictorially represented in "BOSTON ILLUSTRATED," in the best style of graphic art.

☞ *The object and character of* "BOSTON ILLUSTRATED" *are so highly approved by the Executive Committee of the Peace Jubilee, that, by a unanimous vote, it is permitted to be sold within the Coliseum, — a compliment and courtesy accorded to no other book.*

Price, Fifty Cents.

JAMES R. OSGOOD & CO., Publishers,

www.ingramcontent.com/pod-product-compliance
Lightning Source LLC
Chambersburg PA
CBHW020240090426
42735CB00010B/1782